DETOUR

One Wrong Turn Can Alter the
Course of Your Life

SHAWNA C. FLIGGINS-BRANCH

Copyright © 2016 by Shawna C. Fliggins-Branch

Detour
One Wrong Turn Can Alter the Course of Your Life
by Shawna C. Fliggins-Branch

Printed in the United States of America.

ISBN 9781498479417

All rights reserved solely by the author. The author guarantees all contents are original and do not infringe upon the legal rights of any other person or work. No part of this book may be reproduced in any form without the permission of the author. The views expressed in this book are not necessarily those of the publisher.

Unless otherwise indicated, Scripture quotations taken from the Holy Bible, New International Version (NIV). Copyright © 1973, 1978, 1984, 2011 by Biblica, Inc.™. Used by permission. All rights reserved.

Scripture quotations taken from the King James Version (KJV) –*public domain.*

Scripture quotations taken from the New King James Version (NKJV). Copyright © 1982 by Thomas Nelson, Inc. Used by permission. All rights reserved.

www.xulonpress.com

Dear Toni,
Greater is ahead!
Look for blessings from the most unlikely places!
Apostle S Branch :)

Foreword

In the eBook, *Inspirational Words of Wisdom for Challenging Times*, there is a quote by Jefferson Bass which says "Each moment of your life is the sum total of all the prior moments. There's not a single thing that happens to you that doesn't leave its mark; doesn't redirect your course somehow; doesn't make you more fully who you are." A detour is one of those moments that can leave a mark in your life for it redirects plans.

Detours can be time consuming, stressful, frustrating, painful and sacrificial; especially for people who are meticulous planners. It wreaks havoc on a carefully planned life. Get a driver's license by age eighteen, complete college by age twenty-two, have a career and be in leadership by thirty, begin a family and have a home before age thirty-five, and the list goes on. When setting life goals, nowhere in your wildest dreams do you anticipate a simple decision (like love) to disrupt your goals or alter your life. After all, such things as love, death, taxes, and sacrifices are a part of life. Anyone who sets a career goal and decides to make a career change is certainly aware that they (and their family) will need to make sacrifices; especially if the career change requires one to leave a well-paying job for an entry-level position. However, that pink-slip (layoff) during the holiday season is an unexpected painful detour which requires immediate redirection and sacrifices. Needless to say, I never experienced this, but I know many who have. My detour was somewhat different.

As I was reading the chapter *God's Permissive Will*, in *Detour* by Shawna Fliggins-Branch my mind returned to my adolescent years in Riviera Beach, Florida. I remember my dream to go to college, become a lawyer, fight for the rights of oppressed people, get married, have children, and live in a nice, affluent neighborhood by the time I was thirty-five years of age. It was my goal to accumulate enough wealth to retire by age fifty-five, enjoy life and not die by the time I was sixty-two years old. In my day it seemed like many people died after working all their lives. It was not going to happen to me. This was during the era of the Civil Rights Movement when young blacks would resonate the atmosphere with, "I'm black and I'm proud." My classmates and I were so confident we would achieve all the plans for our lives once we left high school (and our parents' homes). I don't think any of us made love a part of the equation. I began to date a schoolmate. The love bug hit me and nothing anyone said could shake my desire to marry my man. My flesh was on fire, my heart alive, my emotions a roller coaster, and my once analytical and straight-forward thinking mind became mush. He and I had all the answers about how we could marry and I still achieve my goals. After all, he and I had similar goals. However, the means of achieving those goals were different. My parents were not in agreement. My mother told me all the sacrifices I would have to make especially as a young black female in tumultuous times. My mother's (and most adults of that day) answer to success was a college education, then a job. Did I listen? Of course I did not.

That way of thinking was old fashioned. We could merge our course of action to obtain life goals. No big deal. So knowing more than my old-fashioned parents I ran away to Texas and got married. Little did I know how my emotions, ego, intelligence, ability to reason and justify my decision would impact my dream and alter my life. One rebellious decision caused me a thirty-four year dream detour. One must realize that during the 1970s and 1980s, we did not have technology or credible on-line colleges like today. There was just so much that this naïve young adult just did not know about life. We did not count on a child coming so soon in the marriage. So now, I have disobeyed my parents, gotten married, and now have a child. This is now a double detour and I must forego my dream of college and becoming a lawyer. I have no regrets. This double detour redirected the course of my life and has contributed to the woman I have become. I am not a lawyer, but I am something more. A born again believer in Christ Jesus, with two beautiful daughters and a call to be a twenty-first

Foreword

century prophetic voice for the Lord. Now I am positioned to mentor, coach and even counsel people to prevent them from needing a lawyer. I agree with Ms. Fliggins-Branch, surely "God Knows All".

In *Detour, "One Wrong Turn Can Alter the Course of Your Life"*, Shawna Fliggins-Branch's spellbounding journey will cause you to laugh, cry, and even say – "That's me". This is not a Sunday School story of Christian rhetoric nor is it a Grimm's fairy tale. It is a true account of an impressionable woman's choice to make a self-fulfilling decision which caused her life to seemingly spiral out of control. For a season (thankfully less than mine) she also had to forego her dream. However, the redirection did not end in defeat. As I read her story, I saw my life and the lives of countless other men and women who have experienced detours. Some are still on detour.

For a moment, like so many of us, Ms. Fliggins-Branch took a detour. She was temporarily off the path, but found the way back to the main road. Her detour was part of the Master molding and making her into a fine vessel fit for His use. He knew the plans that He had for her. This is a story of faith, courage and hope for those who have or will experience a detour from their well-planned life. So, I leave you now to read her story. A story for those about to make a decision that could alter the course of their life.

Prophet Karen E. McCray, D.Min.
Oil for Joy Ministry
Gwynn Oak, MD

Acknowledgments

My heartfelt gratitude goes to:

Almighty God. Without you Father, I would be nothing. I had absolutely no clue where this journey would go and so many times I felt that I would die in the midst of it, but you have kept me, protected me, instructed me and guided me by your Holy Spirit. My choices led me down a dark path, yet you never left me or allowed me to be destroyed. Instead, our relationship has become greater and even more personal. I am so humbled that in spite of it all you still call me your child.

To my late husband, Mr. Bobby Lee Branch, without whom this story would not have been possible. Bobby, you taught me so much. You allowed your weaknesses to be used to give me strength, knowledge and wisdom in those areas where I was most naive. You taught me to be strong and to pay close attention to the things and people around me. I am thankful for the time we had together and that God allowed you to pass my way. Bobby, I will never forget you. R.I.P.

To my mother, Ms. Ida Elaine Fliggins, for your love, support and encouragement. Thank you for raising me to love and serve God. You instilled in me the importance of living holy and allowing God to have full reign of my life. Your labor of love has paid off. I love and appreciate you.

To my friends and sisters, Deborah Blassingame and Prophet Karen E. McCray. Ladies, thank you for the *push* to finish this project. Your prayers and constant reminder of what God told me to do has brought me to the completion of this book. Thank you for your obedience to God concerning me.

To my cousin Edwina Bell, there were times along the way that I had to find refuge and you opened your doors to me. I am eternally grateful for your love and support. You've always treated

Acknowledgments

me with respect and never judged me. Thank you so much! I love you dearly.

Apostle-Bishop Anthony Fliggins, Sr., my uncle and his wife, **Evangelist Ida Mae Fliggins**, thank you so much for everything that you have done to help me. Your love and support is greatly appreciated. Thank you Uncle Anthony for always reminding me of what God said and helping me to stay encouraged. You never gave up on me and I appreciate you so much.

To my new sister and coach, Evangelist Cheryle T. Ricks, author of *Sister Circle: The Power of Sisterhood*. You have written an awesome book. Thank you for unselfishly sharing information and tips with me and for encouraging me through this project.

To my family, the Fliggins Family. What a great legacy we have. We are a people of greatness and I am honored to be a part of this family.

To my church family, Kingdom Workers International Ministries. Thank you for your love, support and respect. I am so thankful to Almighty God for sending all of you to the ministry. It is through you that I am challenged daily to be my best, do my best and to become all that God has called me to be. I always want to be a good Godly example for you and to show you that anything is possible with God. I could not imagine this time of my life without each of you.

To you, the reader: Thank you for supporting me by purchasing this book. I am glad that you took the time to invest in yourself and/or someone you know and love. This book was written by inspiration from God to encourage and help you. I pray that you will enjoy it, be enlightened and have a life changing experience as you read this book. Be encouraged in all that you do. God loves you and so do I. God bless you!

There are so many others that have been instrumental in the molding and shaping of my life, past and present. From my great grandmother, Ida I. Lancaster and my grandmother, Mary E. Simmons; to my godparents Elder W.W. Covington & Mrs. Mable Covington, who were instrumental in the shaping and molding of my spiritual foundation. All of whom have gone home to be with the Lord.

Acknowledgments

To school teachers, counsellors, pastors, and the list goes on. I was very sheltered as a child and I couldn't understand why, but as I take a look back on those who were a part of my formative years I can say that I am thankful for the things that I was taught and for the great impartation of lessons well learned.

As we go through this journey of life there are many key players to help create the story called, "Your Life". I am thankful for every person that has been and is a part of my life today because my story is still being written. It is not possible to name every person one by one, so if you are reading this book and know that God has placed you in my life please know that I'm speaking to you when I say, "Thank you."

God has given me a most precious gift...the opportunity to minister to His people and to be a living example of His undying, unfailing mercy and grace. This project has caused me to relive memories that I had filed way back in my mind. Although it has taken me so long to release this small portion of the story, I am happy to finally share what God has given me. I believe it will open many eyes, answer questions, cause many to think and consider their choices and actions, as well as remind many that no matter what you've done or been through, God is a keeper and through Him all things are possible.

Contents

Foreword	v
Acknowledgments	xi
Introduction	xix
God Knows All	23
"I Got This"	31
The Birthing of a Gift	32
Tell the Story	46
The Safest Place	58
"Not My Will"	64
God's Permissive Will	65
Happily Ever After?	71
How Did I Get to This Place?	77
A Divinely Orchestrated Diversion	89
"I'm Ready, Lord"	98
It's Time to Turn Around	99
Restoration Has Come	106

Introduction

Have you ever been driving down the highway, heading on a nice long road trip? Excitement is in the air. You have not been on a vacation in quite some time and now you finally have that opportunity to get away by yourself and to yourself. Whew! It does not get any better than this. You have your directions all mapped out, printed and lying on the seat next to you. You do not have a GPS system, so of course you are relying on what you have printed from MapQuest. As you are safely going along, singing with your favorite CD playing, tapping your fingers on the steering wheel and periodically reaching over for a snack, you suddenly begin to see those all too familiar orange and black signs along the road that say, "Detour Ahead."

Detour

Oh no! A detour! What? It is late at night! You prefer traveling at night because there is less traffic at night and so traveling at that time is more fun for you because you have the open road pretty much all to yourself. Sure, you may have to share the highway with a few truck drivers, but there is still plenty of road for everybody. It is way past the evening rush hour and a long time before the morning rush, so you say to yourself, "I'm good. Highway, here I come!" Now, out of nowhere, you are faced with a detour! Ugh!

Well, you keep driving because of course you cannot turn back. You are in the middle of the highway. The only way for you to go is forward and you see another sign, "Detour 2 Miles Ahead."

"Awww...man," you say to yourself, "I sure hope this doesn't take me too far out of my way! I hope they don't send me on some obstacle course and get me lost! They better have signs to direct me right back to the main road!" Yet you keep driving ahead and suddenly there it is, that big orange and black

Introduction

sign, this time joined by a huge arrow pointing to the right which says, "Detour Here." So here you are. You are now in the detour zone. You drive for a while and realize how deserted and dark this road is. Sure, there are a few lights along the road, but it is not as bright as the main road. It is quiet and it is lonely. Not many people out because, remember, you left during a time when there would not be many people on the road. So, you are faced with a harsh reality, "I'm on this long, dark road all by myself." A twinge of fear goes through your stomach, but you are not too worried because there should be another sign coming up soon to further direct you along this path. While driving along for what seems like forever, you begin to wonder, "When will I see another sign to direct me towards the way back to the road I was on and, better yet, where is this detour taking me?"

You drive for what seems to be another twenty-five miles and finally you see another sign which says, "Exit here for the detour." So you take the exit, hoping that you will be led back to familiar territory. The night is lonely and still, but you hold on to hope that you are finally back on the right track. As you glance at the clock on the dashboard, you are terrified to realize that you had been redirected by a detour that has taken you more than one and a half hours to travel, "What? How is that possible? This trip is so simple. I travel this way all the time! Why now? Why did they have to put a detour in effect tonight of all nights?! Lord, please just help me to find my way back to the place where I belong. Please!"

Suddenly, mixed with all of the other emotions that you have already experienced like fear, frustration, and annoyance, you are now confused. Confused because although you have taken the exit that the detour sign led you to take, you find that you are just as far away from your destination as you were almost two hours ago. You have driven all this time and traveled such a long way only to find out that you are no closer than you were before the detour took place. How is that possible? All that driving? The detour should have taken you around and brought you further up the road, closer to your destination. How could you still be so far behind? So far off course?

God Knows All

What is a detour? The Merriam-Webster Dictionary defines a detour as: "(1) the act of going or traveling to a place along a way that is different from the usual or planned way; (2) a road, highway, etc, that you travel on when the usual way of traveling cannot be used; (3) a deviation from a direct course or the usual procedure; especially: a round-about way temporarily replacing part of a route."

The subject matter discussed in this book will follow the thought behind meaning number three: A deviation from a direct course or the usual procedure. I want to talk to you about taking detours in your life. My effort is to show you how our decisions and choices can cause us to deviate from the original, direct course that we were created for and that was divinely chosen for us by God. We end up going a round-about way which leads us down a long, troublesome road, causing years of unwanted and unnecessary delays to reaching our destiny.

Detours; unpredictable, uncomfortable, unwelcomed, yet we are sometimes forced to take them. Detours can occur anytime, anywhere and for many reasons, but no matter what the reason a detour will definitely alter the course that you were originally on and will not always lead you to where you were originally headed. At least not without a series of unwanted twists and turns. Funny thing about detours though; they are not always thrust on us, nor do they always show up out of nowhere. In life, we will consciously make a series of decisions and choices that will change the course of our lives one way or the other; sometimes for the better, but yet too often for the worse.

As we grow up and begin to take control of our lives, we will do what we want to do, say what we want to say, go where we want to go and be with whomever we decide to be with. However, not every decision we make will be the one that God had divinely prepared for us and when we choose to go against His will for our lives, we take a major, life changing *detour*! We deviate from our heavenly Father's plan.

Jeremiah 29:11 says, "For I know the thoughts that I think toward you, says the LORD, thoughts of peace and not of evil, to give you a future and a hope." (NKJV)

God has, in all of His infinite wisdom, planned a wonderful life for each of us and in this life He has given us free will. Trouble is, as we grow from childhood into adulthood we take hold of this life we have been blessed with and begin to govern it the way we choose without consulting the One who gave us this life in the first place, which is God, our Father and Creator. If, in fact, Almighty God has created us and given us life, wouldn't it make sense that He knows what we should do with it? After all, He only wants the best for us and wants to bless us.

Humans are something else! When we grab hold of a concept or idea that we are very passionate about, we will do anything we have to do to make that thing happen — good, bad or indifferent. We put a lot of time and energy into doing what we want to do to achieve whatever outcome we have decided that we want to achieve, and oftentimes we have not considered the consequences of our actions. Think about this scenario: A man has decided that he is interested in a woman and has planned out the entire relationship in his mind. He feels he knows how he will approach her, how she will respond, what he expects her to do for him or how she will fall for him once he makes his request known. "I believe we belong together."

Sounds good, doesn't it? What's wrong with being attracted to someone and expressing those feelings to her? Well, the picture I just painted for you involves two individuals, one who has made the decision and has developed this relationship already in his head and an innocent victim who has no clue what is coming her way. Still, where is the problem? Well, the problem is that our pursuer is pursuing after someone who is unavailable! She is not free to enter into a relationship with our pursuer because she is already happily involved with her spouse or significant other. Yet our pursuer is determined to make this thing happen. Caution signs are everywhere, "Do Not Pass Go!", "Stop Here", "Do Not Enter", "Dead Zone." All the signs are directing this person another way, but because he is determined to have who he wants, he must proceed although there are warning signs everywhere.

Our pursuer has decided to take a detour off of the main road, the safe road and travel down a road that has been blocked off. This detour is bound to be detrimental not only for our pursuer, but to their person of interest and the one they are already committed to, but because we are beings that must have what we want no matter what the circumstances, we will proceed anyway and decide to let the chips fall where they may. In life there are stops signs and if you go through the stop sign you have the potential to have a major or tragic accident.

Unfortunately, we live in a time where there are some who do not respect the sanctity of marriage or platonic relationships, so in this instance our pursuer may get by with it, but I believe that there are many people who still believe in doing things the right way, God's way, and thus their respect and love for their spouses will cancel any pursuits that come. They have eyes only for the one that they have committed their lives to and they will not do anything to cross the line, no matter what is dangled in front of them to entice them. Yea! I congratulate those people and pray God's continued blessings upon them and I pray for those who have yet to come to that understanding.

God said to Jeremiah, "I know the plans I have for you….." How many of us really understand that God knows exactly what He has planned for us? He created us on purpose, for a purpose and with purpose. You are not a mistake, so whatever your life was to be, God is the one in charge of that. One of the main reasons many of us find ourselves taking detours in life is because we lack patience and do not want to wait on God.

Psalm 27:14 "Wait on the LORD: be of good courage, and He shall

strengthen thine heart: wait, I say, on the LORD," (KJV).

This passage of scripture is not just making a suggestion, it is a statement of encouragement, strong advice and warning because the writer understood that when we do not wait on the Lord, but instead choose to take matters into our own hands we can, and most times will, mess things up. He understood that although we may think we know what is best for us, we really do not. Pursuing after things and people that God never intended for us to be involved in or with can lead down a bad road and so the writer is urging us to wait on God. We are also being encouraged to wait on the Lord because He knows what is ahead. He sees and knows what we cannot see and do not know.

God, our Creator, had our lives completely mapped out long before He formed the earth, and so when He sees us going down the wrong path He sends warnings and puts up those stop signs. All too often we ignore Him and proceed anyway, only to find out later that He was trying to save us from something. We are being encouraged to wait because even the writer himself came to know that God would not cause a delay or deny us anything because He did not want us to enjoy our lives. He does it because He loves us and wants the best for us. Since God knows everything about us, we should trust that if He says, "No," then it is for our good.

I Got This

It's not that I don't trust you, Lord
It's just that I also have a plan
This life that you have given me,
I'm able to take command!

Come on, God, let me show you
I know exactly what to do
Didn't you give me the power of free will
Ok, so again, I know what to do!

I got this, God
I really do
You'll see I'll get it right
I got this...I really do
It's all good...and it's gonna be all right!

Shawna C. Branch

The Birthing of a Gift

During the course of our lives we will make many decisions and those decisions will not always be the best or the right ones to make. I understand what it means to have your life going in one direction and then to make a decision, a detour, that can alter your course. My story is a very intimate one and in order to help you understand how our decisions can be damaging to us if not carefully entered into, I am willing to become transparent and share some of the details of my life that I have never shared before. This topic is so important to me and I want you, the reader, to be blessed and encouraged, yet convicted enough to consider what you choose to do with your life because it can take a very long time to get back on track once you have gotten off on the wrong road.

So, let us start at the beginning. God gifted me with the talent and love for writing at an early age and by the time I was in elementary school I was writing poems, short stories, and the lyrics to songs. I would write about pretty much anything because I just loved to write. I often attribute my love for writing not just as a gift from God, but a forced development from my mother whom I lovingly call "Fliggy". You see, whenever my mother wanted to punish me she would do one of two things: Whip my butt or make me write 1,000 sentences. Sometimes I would get both punishments, but that "1,000 sentence" assignment is the one that I truly believe helped to develop my love for writing and the punishment always fit the crime.

If I was caught talking in school or in church, then I had to write 1,000 times, "I must not talk in school," or, "I must not talk in church." Mom would buy me packs and packs of loose leaf paper at the beginning of the school year and sometimes even at Christmas, so there was no running out and she made me use it, too. So here I go writing my 1,000 sentences to fit whatever punishment was appropriate at the time, (e.g. I must not sleep in church; I must not steal; I must not play in school; etc.).

Needless to say that this task, while mean and cruel to me at the time, began to become strangely entertaining and fun because, again, something so much more substantial was being developed. Anyway, here I am deep in the midst of a written punishment which has become my secret, personal friend because each day after school when my homework was done I had to "spend time with my sentences." They became my friend and intrigued my alter ego; my imagination! Oh yes, I have a very vivid imagination and a very creative mind. It is part of my innate nature, the way I was created by Almighty God.

So this punishment that should have made me mad that I could not be outside playing, began to become fun to me and I would often create games with it. Sometimes I wrote a full page of "I's" all in a row or start at the end of the sentence and write a full row of the word "school". I might write a full page of half a sentence then go back to the top and write the end of the sentence. In other words, I would come up with variations to create fun for myself and make the experience more creative. I would repeat each sentence as I wrote it and give myself time challenges to see how fast I could finish a certain amount.

After a while I began to finish these sentence punishments faster than Mom expected and I think she realized that this was no longer sufficient because I began to develop a love for it. A love for writing a thousand sentences? No, but rather a love for writing itself! Through this act of discipline, a talent was born and an innate, God-given gift was discovered. Shawna loves to write! So, I began to write more and more. I attended school in Brooklyn, New York and while in the sixth grade at Public School 262, I entered into any activity that involved writing or storytelling. I recall one storytelling contest that I entered. I cannot fully remember how many students participated, but I do remember my story: "Henny Penny" by Paul Galdone. I loved this story and memorized the whole book in a short time. The contest required that you not only memorize it word for word, cover to cover, but that you were able to show expression of each character, be realistic or creative in your delivery and, of course, you could not make any mistakes.

It was so exciting to me and I worked on that story as much and as hard as I could because I wanted to win that contest. On the day of the contest I was very nervous, but excited and confident because my mom had helped me so much and I could repeat that story in my sleep! I would recite it to anyone who would listen. I had worked so hard and was ready to do my best. Well, I will tell you that when my turn came I stood and told my story to the best of my ability. I had fun with it, too, making expressions and sounding like the different animals in the story. I did well but I did make a couple of mistakes and instead of winning first place, I came in second. Aww, man! I was so disappointed because I knew this story! How could I mess up? Even so, my mom was so proud of me because I had tried and although I did not win first place, she told me that I had done a wonderful job and that second place was still great.

My writing continued to get better as time went on. I participated in a lot of writing events in school. Needless to say, my favorite subject was English. Anything to do with writing, telling stories, poetry, plays, words, punctuation, grammar, etc. was my love and passion. I always received my highest grades in English and Math. This trend continued throughout my elementary school years and at my sixth grade graduation I received the greatest honor and biggest surprise of my young life.

During my sixth grade graduation ceremony, special awards and certificates were being given out to students who had excelled in certain areas during their tenure at P.S. 262. As I sat and listened to the names of the different students being called out to receive one award or another, all of a sudden I heard the announcer say a "Certificate for Creative Writing is being awarded to Shawna C. Fliggins." Oh my goodness, I was in shock! I barely remembered getting out of my seat and going to the stage to receive my award. Oh my goodness! I had been rewarded for something that I loved to do and it had been recognized by the whole school! My mother and my godparents, Elder Woodrow Wilson and Mrs. Mable Covington, were so proud of me that day and I remember thinking, "*Wow*, did I really just win an award for creative writing?" What an exciting thing for an eleven-year old.

This continued as I moved from grade to grade. It was during my middle school years that I began to write plays. I was honored to have them performed at the church that we were attending at that time. I would write plays for different holidays and programs. I also loved acting as a child and would perform in many church and school plays. My love for writing poetry began to develop during middle school as well. I had learned about the different forms of poetry and enjoyed practicing by writing my own poems in the styles that I had learned.

My gift and talent for writing went to another level during high school. I remember very fondly one instance in particular when I was sixteen years old. My science teacher had given us a project that most of us did not want to do. So one day he decided to threaten us. I really think it was a bluff, and he said, "If you don't do the project, then you have to write me a book!" What? Write a book?! *All right, I can do that*, I thought to myself. Anything to get out of the science project. I really did not like science much anyway, so it was on.

I went home from school that day and got right to work. I thought and thought about what to write about. Well, you know how teenagers are. So, of course during that time I had a terrible crush on one of the young guys at church. What better storyline than that? I came up with a title, *Torn Between Girls*, and got busy. Of course it would take me several weeks to get it done, so once I realized that I really had something going here I went to my teacher and told him what I was doing. He gave me one month to get it done, and of course I was up for the challenge. My mom was so surprised when she realized that I was actually writing a book. She told me later that she did not know what I was doing, only that she thought I had a lot of homework to do. She became such a great source of encouragement for me and

The Birthing of a Gift

she was proud that I had taken on the challenge. I worked on that book every day and boy, oh boy, was it coming together.

I had a friend at church who could draw quite well and so I asked him to illustrate the cover for me. My best friend's mom would be the editor and she also typed up the final copy that was to be submitted to my teacher. Once the book was complete, she proofread it for me and typed it up. I was on a roll. I do realize that I made one big mistake during that process, though. I had let a few of my close friends at church read portions of the book and since they all knew how I felt about this person, they could easily figure out the main characters in the story. I felt a little embarrassed about it at the time, but I did not let it bother me too much. I was just so excited about my book. The villain in the story was another young lady who also liked him at the time, but what made me upset was that he liked her, too. So, my fantasy caused her to be the bad girl in the book and of course I got the man! Hahahaha! Boy, this is funny now that I am thinking about it twenty-nine years later. Help me, Lord!

Anyway, back to the main point here. I finished the book in time to meet my one-month deadline and turned it in to my teacher. He was surprised to see that I had finished it in the time frame he had given and said he would read it and get back to me. It took him about two weeks and finally he asked my mother to come in for a meeting. When Mom came to the school to meet with him he began to tell her how impressed he was that I had accepted the challenge to write the book. He further told her that I had a great talent for writing and that he could see me having a bright future in it. At the close of the meeting he made this announcement, "Ms. Fliggins, I am giving Shawna the highest grade I can, but I can't give her a 100% because I think she is already a professional writer and has written books before." My mom said, "No. This is her first time ever writing a book." He continued, "Well, this is really good, but I'm going to give her a 95% and encourage her to continue writing." He gave us the book back and I left his classroom on top of the world! Although we could not fully understand why he would not give me the perfect grade, we knew that he was quite impressed and that something great had been developed.

As I reflect on that experience now, I believe that my teacher's reason for not giving me a perfect grade on that assignment was a way of saying, "I know you've got what it takes, but if I let you feel you have already reached your pinnacle, you may not continue to pursue your writing with the mindset of perfecting or polishing what you have started." Truly, there was so much more that I could still aspire to in this field. Sometimes when we are given too much praise too soon, we tend to feel that we have "made it" and thus we can slip into a mode of pride. Pride can keep you from doing your best and becoming the best that you can become. It can keep you from reaching out to those who have more experience than you have and give you the false impression that you are so good that no one can tell you anything. Pride will cause you to miss out on great opportunities.

My mom and I were so excited about the book. My teacher said that it was really good! My friends, my editor and a few others thought it was great, so now we thought: Why not try to have it published?

I did some research and got information on a few publishing companies and submitted the manuscript to one of them. When I got the response I was so ecstatic! They really liked the manuscript and wanted to publish it, but it would cost well over $1,000 to complete the publishing process. Well, we were not the most financially stable family, so $1,000 sounded like a life's savings for us and since we did not understand at the time how to really promote what I had done to get help with the costs, publishing the book became a distant dream that has yet to become a reality twenty-nine years later. Wow!

    I know I have gone a long way back, but trust me, I am heading somewhere. My endeavor is to share some worthy and much needed nuggets along the way. I want to pause here and say that when you have a dream, never let that dream sit and tarry too long. Try all you can to make your dreams become a reality. We did not understand how to do that then and no one, not anyone we knew, helped to birth it out by sharing helpful tips or information to guide us along.

So, there it was, a nicely written novel, written by a sixteen-year old girl. A product with the potential to make us a lot of money was tucked safely away in a box with the possibility of never being published. *Do not let your dreams collect dust! Strive to make them a reality.* Time goes by so fast and before you know it, years have slipped by. Whew...that is a teary thought, yet an unnerving truth.

Parents, I share this encouraging advice with you: If you see that your child has a special gift or talent, do all that you can to nurture and channel that gift early because you never know where it could lead.

Tell the Story

In January 2011, I had a very heartfelt conversation with my late husband, Bobby Lee Branch. We talked about several things, including how God had called me to the ministry and anointed me and how He was going to greatly use me in the kingdom. Then Bobby began to apologize to me for causing so much trouble in our marriage due to his drug addiction and he told me that he never meant to hurt me. He encouraged me to go forth, to run and be all that God has called me to be. Before we hung up the phone he said to me these words, "Shawna, you have a powerful testimony and it's going to bless and deliver many people. You must tell your story."

I said, "Yes, *we* do have a powerful testimony." He said, "But you have to tell it. Tell our story." Tears began to fill my eyes and I wondered how and when I would tell it. I thought it would come through a play, but each time I tried to write it, it did not quite come together because the intensity of the memories was overwhelming. I would have to stop because I could not push past some of the pain of losing him, yet I knew that one day I would have to tell this story.

The other reason why it has been hard to write this book is because of the truths that I would have to face about some things. Being transparent about your personal life is not always easy for some of us. You see, many times as we go through life we will get to that crossroad of knowing the truth about a situation, but we have a hard time facing up to those truths so we keep moving on and on hoping that we will not have to ever deal with admitting what we know the real truth is. I hope that makes sense to you.

I have lived every day of my life with the reality of a choice that I made over fifteen years ago and it has not always been easy to admit my mistakes but, as my Bobby said, I must tell the story. This book is entitled *Detour* because it directly details a decision that I made in 2001 that has truly altered the course of my life up to this present time, but by the mercy of God I have been sustained and I know and believe that better and greater is coming!

I shared in the previous chapter of how I progressed with my writing from a young girl and that by the age of sixteen years old I had written my first novel. Well, my pursuit of writing did not stop there. I continued to write and write some more throughout my teenage years and even as I entered into college. I can remember one of my college professors telling me that I had a great future as a writer, author or journalist. My writing skills intrigued my English professors and some said that "I had a way with words." This trend continued as I entered into my twenties, writing poems, short stories, plays, etc. I just loved to write.

During the mid-1990's, my family (Mom and I) went through a very traumatic, very hurtful experience which led to public shame and although the situation was due to false accusation and lies, it brought great damage and disgrace to my family. This situation angered me and for the first time in my life I knew what it felt like to want to literally kill someone.

I was angry, disgusted, furious, and bitter. It really brought out a bad side of me. I began to hate people whom at one time I had deeply loved and cared about and for whom I would have done anything. People that we had fed, clothed, and housed. My goodness! It was a blow from which we would take years to recover. We experienced people turning against us and lying on us to be in cahoots with other people they felt were better than us. We were mistreated, cast aside, ostracized, and pretty much told that we were no longer welcomed in the one place that we used to feel the safest and freest–church.

A shocker? Well, it has been happening all the time and it is still happening today. Years are moving on, times are changing, but people have not changed much. There are still professional liars in the church and people who will always go along with them. I am not about to get on the topic of church-hurt, as they call it because then I would have to change the title of the book, but trust me, I know all too well about the subject.

Anyway, this situation affected my family so much so that we were forced to leave the church.

Detour

Our world was shattered, to say the least. Needless to say, going to church after that was pretty much out of the question for a while. We just stopped going and when you have been raised in church all of your life and that is pretty much all you know, to wake up on a Sunday morning knowing that you have no church to go to — not by choice, but by force — is a very horrible reality, but that is what we had to do.

My hatred and bitterness began to take me to a very dark place in my mind. It grew to the point that one day I asked my co-worker if he knew any hit men. He looked at me as if I had a few heads and said, "What? Do you have any idea what you're saying?" I said, "Yes." He replied, "No, you don't, and this is not the Shawna that *I* know, talking." Mind you, he was not saved. That day, for the first time I shared the experience with someone because until that time I was so numb and embarrassed that I could barely talk to anyone. My everyday was like a nightmare and I lived in a haze.

After sharing the experience with him, he encouraged me to hold on to my faith, the faith that I had been witnessing to him about, and the trust in God that I had told him he needed to have. He then told me about his uncle, who was pastor of a large church in Brooklyn, and told me to go visit. In fact, when I did decide to go he went with me and introduced me to his uncle. I enjoyed myself there, but was not about to commit to another church. I did continue to visit from time to time.

God is so awesome. When you have a destined purpose and a mandate on your life, it does not matter what terrible, horrifying things you go through in life, nothing can stop your destiny. Eventually, I began visiting different churches, but could not make a connection. I could not find peace and I could not rest. Every day, my mind was consumed with the situation and the hurt that it had caused my family. I was sick inside. This issue went on from the year 1995 into the year 1996 and it sometimes got ugly. There were court sessions and all kinds of legal things to deal with and face.

During that time, I was working as a clerk for the New York State Insurance Fund in Manhattan, New York. One day when I got to work I sat at my desk, turned on my computer and instead of getting right to work, I began to type. My God! Thank you, Jesus. At that point, and I really did not realize it then, but thinking back on it now over twenty years later, writing was not only my passion and my love, but it was about to become my therapy.

I started typing and began to write a play. Of course, the theme was centered around my pain and the pain of my family. I began to write my signature play, "Murderers!" The main idea of the story is how church people murder one another with their tongues through gossip and slander and it is based on Psalm 52:2, "Thy tongue deviseth destruction; like a razor, working deceitfully." I had heard my mother say it one day: "All church folks do is murder one another with their tongues!" Those words stuck with me and became the main idea of my newest project — a full length, three act musical drama.

I really had no clue what I was writing at the time, but I just kept typing and I began to see this manuscript formulate and come together. I realized, "Wow! I've got something here."

Every day after that I spent time working on that play. I would get to work one or two hours early and stay late most afternoons just so I could work on this play. God would filter the words, scenes, names, and locations. He was really using me to write this story.

This play became my hope and although the storyline was slightly different, the character would sustain just as much humiliation and pain as my real family did. Something so wonderful and great was about to come out of my pain. I cannot remember exactly how long it took me to complete the play, but I know it was not more than two months. It came together quickly because I was fixed and focused; besides the words that God was filtering to me came so easily and I put it together just the way He showed me.

While writing the play I began to do some research about how to produce the play. How would I get people to be in it? I felt that it was going to be a big production! One of my co-workers whom I had told about the play told me how to copyright the manuscript once it was done to protect it from being used or stolen by anyone else. So once the script was done I had it copy written and then I had to figure out what to do next. I decided to show it to my pastor. Oh yes, by this time I had joined another church. I asked him to read it and tell me what he thought about it. When he was done reviewing it he told me that he loved it and gave me permission to ask certain young people if they would like to be in it.

Well, as things go when you have a vision for something, not everyone will catch on and so I had to leave them alone due to lack of interest, commitment, and dedication. You see, this was not just another little church play. God had blessed me to write a full-length, three act play which included dance renditions and music, so I needed people who were serious about the arts to help me produce this play. Besides that, this was a representation of the hell and hurt my family had experienced. This was important to me and it had to be done right!

One of my good friends told me about auditioning people to be in the play and that I could put an ad in the paper. Oh, my goodness. It was really happening now. I got all the information I could get, placed the ad and before I knew it people were responding. I also decided to start my own production company, Higher Dimensions Productions, and began to audition real, experienced and aspiring actors for the new original gospel play, "Murderers!" Written, directed and produced by Shawna C. Fliggins. I was both excited and deathly afraid.

The process of auditioning potential cast members was very interesting. I had absolutely no experience and no real clue about what I was doing, so I would ask questions and do research so that I could appear knowledgeable when the actors came to the studio to audition. It is so funny how you try to appear to know what you are doing and God helps you to look your best even though you have no clue.

On the day of the first auditions for the play, I met several candidates. Many of them had prior experience and knew the routine, but some were brand new to the acting scene so they did not understand much about how the process worked. That day I met people like Quan'Asia Bain-James, a young woman who had a lot of acting experience. She had performed in several plays and acted in a couple of movies with well-known producers. In fact, several of the candidates that I met that day had performed in plays and other film work as well.

Detour

Also that first day, a young lady came in with her son and when I came to interview him I asked her name first and she said, "Angela Williams, and this is my son Tyler J. Williams." Oh my goodness, he was so cute! He was small, about four years old, with a head full of curly hair. Tyler was so smart. I was told that he had auditioned for another play, but had not done any work yet. I gave him a portion of script to read and study for a while before I interviewed him. When it was his turn to audition he did it so well and just like I asked him to do it. I was surprised to see that he had actually memorized the portion of script that was previously given to him. I knew that day that I would hire Tyler to be in the play. He performed with us for close to two years and then hit stardom after signing with a well known casting agency in New York City. He is now known as Tyler James Williams. I am sure you have heard of him from "Everybody Hates Chris," The Disney Channel and a multitude of commercials, television shows, movies, music, etc. During their time with my production group his mom, Angela, became my stage manager. God allowed us to embrace one another as sisters and friends and He used her to encourage me in so many areas of my life. I am proud to have worked with these wonderful people. Each of them has added so many wonderful things to my life.

I had to do a couple of auditions to get a good cast of people, but by the time it was done God had blessed me with a great group of actors and for those who have had the opportunity to see the play, I am sure they can attest that these actors were truly talented. "Murderers!" was performed in the New York City area from 1996 to 1999 and I must say it went quite well.

Certainly this was the beginning of something successful and wonderful. I still had much to learn, but I was off to a great start. So what happened? With all of the prophecies spoken over me, my gift for writing, my productions, why am I not at *that* place of prosperity, not living in Hollywood or at least running a progressive theatrical business? One word answers that question: **Detour!**

The Safest Place

One Sunday during the latter portion of 2014, I was riding in a van with a few people and we were headed to church. We were driving down E. North Avenue in Baltimore, Maryland and without warning we noticed that the street was blocked off just past the traffic light near North and Greenmount Avenues. Police cars and fire trucks had blocked the road and we had to make a detour. Now, there were no signs warning us that the road was blocked nor was there an indication that a detour had to be made, so none of us were aware until we got stuck looking at a closed road. A little frustrated, the driver immediately had to figure out which way to go. The rest of us in the vehicle were trying to help by making suggestions.

The Safest Place

"Turn left here and you should come to a street and be able to go around."

"I don't know the name of the street, but maybe it leads to another street and then we can make another left and get back to the road we were on."

All of these suggestions, but none of us were completely sure where we were going and although this area was familiar to us, for a while we felt slightly confused. We began to discuss how silly it was that there were no signs warning people about this detour. In all of this I thought about all of the other cars that had done the same thing and one car after another, we all had to turn around and find another way to go.

While we were driving, we kept talking about trying to find our way back to the main street again to hurry and get to our destination, because now we were late. I also realized that at the point where we had to make the detour we were only a few blocks from where we were heading. Just then this took me into a place of deep thought. Oftentimes we are well on our way towards our destiny or our next level. Success could be right around the corner, but something or someone can come to throw us off course and if we are not paying attention we will find ourselves diverting off of that straight path and making a turn that will leave us confused and frustrated and cause us to arrive to our destination a lot later than planned. Well, we did finally get to the church fifteen minutes late, but thank God we arrived there safely.

I do realize that not every detour that happens in our lives is necessarily our fault, but whatever it was can certainly delay your plans, your goals and your appointment with success. It is true, you may eventually achieve your goal and realize that dream, for really the key is in not giving up, but have you ever wondered what life could be like now if the choices you made then were different? An ungodly, un-ordained diversion in the divine plan of God for your life can delay your blessings for years and one day you will look back and say, "I should have done this years ago," or, "I should have achieved this degree years ago," or, "Why am I still broke and financially strapped? I should be doing better than this!" The torture goes on and on. That valley called "What if?" can take you to a place of depression, especially when you look at those you started out with and see their success and how far they have gotten in life; their dreams realized, their goals reached and yours not. It is a bad feeling, yes it is, but let's not make that another detour in our lives. Do not go down the road of self-pity.

When you wake up and realize that you are not yet where you thought you would be or should be, that is the time to grab hold of God like never before and with all boldness and courage you need to declare, "I may not be where I want to be, but I'm not going to give up!" The enemy will speak to your mind and try to make you believe that it is too late, that you have wasted so much time, that it will never happen, that you are stupid, and so on and so on. That is the time to get up and get busy and to declare that your latter days shall be greater than your former days. You can take the lessons that you have learned over the years and still make your dreams come true. It is not over until God says it is over. So be encouraged and get moving. God is all knowing. Do you really think that our Almighty God did not know that you and I would sometimes make bad or wrong choices? Of course He knew and He was there all the time while we were in our mess ups, but He never left us and just like He was there then, He is with us now.

When you make up your mind to do what He told you to do, God is right there ready, willing and able to help you achieve your goals. Whatever He spoke over us in the beginning of time still stands today and it can still come to pass. Trust God, take one step at a time and remind yourself that "He that has begun a good work in me shall perform it until the day of Jesus Christ. I can be all that God said I can be." Hallelujah! Thank you, Jesus.

Excuse me while I give my God thanks. He has truly kept me and been patient with me. When I look back over my life, I realize that there have been so many times when I said, "Lord, thy will be done," but then I made decisions to do what I wanted to do and even prayed specific prayers that things would turn out the way I wanted them to turn out. Then God in His infinite wisdom would allow His permissive will to be done. Why? Not because He did not love me, but if I had never experienced His permissive will, I would never understand the tremendous blessing of walking in His perfect will!

The Safest Place

Oh, my Lord! There is nothing like the perfect will of God. God will keep you and sustain you in His permissive will — that is His grace — but the true glory of God is revealed in your life when you are in walking in His perfect will. There is nothing like it. Doors are opened in His perfect will, supernatural doors! Healing, true anointing, true power. Your real talents and gifts are expressed in His perfect will because He causes all things to become just as He predestined them to be for your life before the beginning of time. It is a place that is often unexplainable because you experience miracles, signs and wonders when you are in His perfect will. It is truly a place to desire to be in and I pray with all diligence that you will learn to accept the perfect will of God for your life, for truly it is the safest place.

Not My Will

Not my will, Dear Lord, but Your will be done
In my life I seek your divine direction and guidance
To walk with You as one.
Yes, I have made my own decisions and choices too
But I have come to clearly realize
That no one knows the course of my life
Or the way I should take but You!

Shawna C. Branch

God's Permissive Will

In the year 2001, I entered into a season of God's permissive will which lasted for ten years.

Earlier I shared with you about how I had started my own production company and began to produce plays. It was a promising time in my life and had I stuck with it there is no telling how things could be going and what my life would be like now. However, it was during that time that I made a decision and chose to take a detour from the path of pursuing my acting and production dream.

Before I go any further, let me say this. As I share these very intimate details of my life I want to first let you know that I share them with full permission of the other person that you will soon come to know as I detail him to you. Other names have been changed or eliminated for the sake of privacy, but this testimony exclusively belongs to me and my late husband. I had his full permission and support to share it. He understood that our testimony would help and bless many people and although he knew he would not be here to see it, again, he told me, "Shawna, you have a powerful testimony. Make sure you tell it and share our story." That was in 2011. It is time for me to tell the story.

In 1993, I became re-acquainted with a childhood friend by the name of Bobby Lee Branch. I had not seen him for twelve years, but when we saw each other again for the first time something inside of me jumped! I was so glad to see him and to know that he was doing well. Over the years I had heard so many things about him, yet deep in my heart I had always held an affection for him that no one was aware of and within a short time of becoming re-acquainted, he and I started dating.

While spending time with Bobby, he would share with me a lot of things that he had experienced over the years since we had seen one another last. I found out that he had spent time in North Carolina with his family, that he had been introduced to drugs at the age of fourteen by one of his cousins that he greatly admired, and so many other things. He shared that he had two children and that at age eighteen he had gotten married, but was soon after divorced. He had been struggling with a drug addiction for several years and was finding it hard to "get clean," as he would say. I would listen to his stories with such interest because they sounded so exciting, like a mystery or adventure. Remember, I am a writer, so a good story will always intrigue me. However, this was not just some fictitious novel he was repeating. This was his life.

After a while of talking and getting to know one another again, we decided to start dating. I recall Bobby calling me one day on the phone and he said, "If I told you that I'm in love with you, what would you say?" I thought about it for a moment. I was both scared and excited all at the same time, but I replied with a calm voice, "I would say that I'm in love with you, too."

He let out a "Yes!" It was a *yes* that said, "I just hit the jackpot!" and I just knew it was accompanied with a huge smile and he laughed. Then he asked if I would be his girlfriend and I said yes. The first person we told was his mother and she was so excited.

Bobby's mother and I had become very close, so when we told her the news she was elated and wished us well, but it would not be that easy with everyone else. As we were moving along in our new relationship, I came to realize that not everyone was jumping for joy. Let me give you some further background here. Bobby and I had grown up in the same church in Brooklyn, New York — Faith Temple Church of God in Christ — where my godparents were the pastor and first lady. My mom had known them while she was living in Baltimore, Maryland, so when she relocated to New York she decided to join their church. Upon arriving at this small, yet fiery holiness church, we came to meet the Branch family, of which Bobby was a part.

Growing up at Faith Temple was quite interesting and fun. We learned a lot from our leaders and they did their best to create a united church family. We, the younger ones, were always together because there were always a lot of church activities that kept us all busy and close.

Although I was five years younger than Bobby, he seemed to always take a liking to me. This I found out years later. I remember one day when I was about eight years old, I was playing and skipping outside in front of the church. I had skipped close to the corner of the block, and somehow all of a sudden I got a piece of glass in my foot. I remember falling to the ground crying and the next thing I knew, Bobby had scooped me up in his arms and took me to my mother who was inside the church. I had no idea where he came from or that he was even watching me, but like Prince Charming he showed up and saved this little damsel in distress. Another fond memory I have of Bobby from our childhood was when I was twelve years old and he had come to help my mom and I move out of an apartment. He was about seventeen at the time. I remember at one point looking out of our living room window and he was sitting on the steps, rocking his head and singing along with some music that was being played very loudly by one of our neighbors. I stood in the window for a while and I remember saying to myself, "I love you, Bobby." After that I did not see him again until I was twenty-four years old.

There were others that we had grown up with who had remained in the same church, and so they knew things about one another. My mom changed membership from Faith Temple when I was twelve years old so I did not keep up with my old friends as much, but by 1993 I had reconnected with a large group of them and so the announcement that Bobby and I were dating was not too well received. Many knew of his drug addiction, his past relationships and such, and they felt that I was making a mistake. I did not pay much attention to them because I had my Prince Charming, and of course I kept reminding myself that I was grown and that I could make my own decisions, never realizing that they were only concerned about me. It is funny, though, how some people will gossip about you, make fun of your situations and make sarcastic remarks all in the hopes of detouring you from making a big mistake or to help change your mind instead of just talking to you and being honest about their concerns and fears for you and the direction you have chosen to take.

Happily Ever After?

On February 5, 2001, I married Bobby Lee Branch in a private ceremony at The River Church in Raleigh, North Carolina. I had relocated to North Carolina in 1999 and Bobby followed about a year and a half later. I was so happy and excited to be his wife. I loved him so much and was glad to finally be able to be with him all the time. I had prayed for this day. I remember it so clearly. I was in my bedroom one day and I cried out to God, "Please Lord, please let me marry him. I love him so much and all I want is for you to give him to me." He did. God permitted it to be so.

We set out to make a life together, and although I continued to receive warnings right up to the day not to marry him, I did it anyway because that was what

I wanted to do. After all, I *was* thirty years old. Who could tell me not to get married? I was still a virgin. I had kept myself. Why couldn't I get married to the man I so desperately loved? Everything was falling right into place. We had found a cozy little place to call home and all was just great...until the monkey showed up.

During the beginning of our marriage I focused a lot on my new family and our home. I stopped writing for a while because there just did not seem to be enough time to focus on it. During the years that Bobby and I were together I had only written a couple of short plays and skits and had only done two small productions, but after a while the desire to write began to grow dim. I would feel a little inspiration, but when I would try to put pen to paper nothing would come out. I had writers' block.

In August of 2004, three years and nine months into our marriage, "the monkey" showed up and Bobby found himself back on drugs. He had been clean and drug free for close to four years when he relapsed, and it was a major shock to my system. I knew nothing about drug addicts. I had no clue of their behaviors, their appetites for the drug, or the great lengths they would go to in order to get it. I had come face to face with a demon that I did not know how to handle. I was completely naive, green and passive at the time; clueless as to what I was about to face.

This drug relapse went on and on for several years and caused our lives to take many horrible turns. In the midst of it all I had completely lost my inspiration and zeal for writing. I was not writing anything. I had put my gift down and had become completely consumed with the fact that my decision to marry this man, this detour that I had chosen to take, had altered my life in a most terrible way. I had no idea how I was going to get out of the mess I had created for myself. Many times I wondered if I would even make it out alive. I had deviated off of the course that God had originally set for me. He permitted it because I wanted it. I had ignored all of the warnings from everyone who seemed to care about me and now my life was a mess. What was I going to do?

This detour that I was on would take me down roads that I would never have imagined I would travel and present me with experiences that I would have never thought of in my wildest dreams. I was constantly reminded that I consciously and knowingly chose the road I was on. I knew what I wanted and where I was heading. I was in the driver's seat and I had control of the wheel. In the beginning. Then it came time that we changed drivers.

Life began to spiral out of control and I realized that *I* was no longer in control, but rather his addiction was. Suddenly I found myself in a very unfamiliar and uncomfortable place. This journey was heading nowhere fast. Crack cocaine and alcohol were now calling the shots and, as hard as I tried to regain control of how the journey was going, I found myself going deeper and deeper down a dark, dismal road that was leading me to the dead zone. I did not grow up around drug addicts. The only time I was ever close to anyone who was intoxicated or high was when I would see them hanging out on the street. Growing up in Brooklyn, New York, it was not strange to see a drunk hung over on the corner. It was the norm, but I did not have to deal with them, let alone live with them.

When two people get married there are so many dreams, goals, ideas, aspirations that are on their minds: where they will live, how to handle the finances, how many children they want to have, and the list goes on. I do not believe anyone gets married with the intention of being abused, mistreated, degraded, separated or divorced. Not most people, anyway. When most young girls dream of getting married they have stars in their eyes from the excitement of planning a wedding, finding the perfect gown, and choosing their bridesmaids. They are not thinking that in just a few short years, life will become a living hell, taking them through a series of abusive experiences that can leave them damaged, depressed, oppressed or worse.

Yet God is so merciful and despite your actions, choices or decisions, when there is a calling on your life and you have been chosen for a specific mandate, nothing can kill you out. Yes, you may go through some bad experiences, but His ultimate plan for your life can still come to pass. On this detour that I had taken I had love, joy and happiness with the man I loved, but all too soon I became the victim of my husband's addiction. He was the addict, but as his wife I suffered the consequences along with him. I went from a happy, blushing bride to a frightened young woman; fearful for my life but worse yet, fearful for my destiny.

This detour took me down so many unwelcomed roads. In the process of living with his addiction I eventually lost everything that I owned. He had sold our cars, furniture, jewelry and many other precious possessions. At one point our home had been turned into a crack house and I found myself living among addicts and alcoholics. Things went from bad to worse until eventually I was left homeless. I was all alone, embarrassed and ashamed, but thanks be to God who always causes us to triumph.

2 Corinthians 2:14 "Now thanks be unto God, which always causeth us to triumph in Christ, and maketh manifest the savor of his knowledge by us in every place." (KJV)

How Did I Get to This Place?

In spite of the challenges that life will present to us as we go along, I am still thankful for this life that God has given me. I am grateful to Him for His mercy and grace towards me. I do not believe that anyone wants to purposely make decisions that can bring harm or detriment to their lives. That is never anyone's original dream from childhood. I cannot imagine a small child in his room playing make believe saying, "Let's pretend that we have made stupid choices and ruined our lives! Doesn't that sound like fun?"

No! On the contrary, as we go along this life there will be many reasons why one would divert from his predestined path and go down the wrong road or simply find himself thrust into a place where he did not expect to be. Even though things happen, we must still take responsibility for our actions, choices and behaviors; not making excuses, but being willing to admit our mistakes, sins and faults and then being courageous enough to do something to change the situation.

In this chapter, I want to share with you some reasons why someone would take a detour in his life. These reasons, of course, relate to those negative choices and aspects of diverting from the ordained path that God has set for us.

Distractions:

A distraction is defined as anything that prevents us from giving something our full attention. Distractions can cause extreme agitation in our minds and our emotions and cause us to lose focus on our goals or targets. When we allow ourselves to become so distracted that we lose focus on what we were supposed to be doing, we are in danger of losing precious time, and before you know it months and even years have gone by and you have not accomplished anything you set out to do.

I must say that not all distractions are bad, but they can become lifelong hindrances if we focus too much time and energy on them instead of learning how to balance it out. For example, you may be a spiritual leader such as a pastor, or a business owner trying to grow a successful business. You are hard working and diligent, but you also have a tendency to allow people to take your focus off of what you need to do for yourself, because every time they "come a callin'" you run to them, put your goals aside and focus on trying to help them out of their situation.

Now, there is absolutely nothing wrong with helping others, please understand me, but if you are not careful by the time you think about doing what you need to do for you, you find yourself exhausted, worn out, frustrated and tired. So now, once again, you have put "you" and your dreams or goals on hold to deal with everything and everybody else. Sometimes we have to say *no* or, "Not right now," so that we can focus on what we need to do.

Who or what distracts you? Consider changing your focus today so that you will not miss fulfilling your own destiny while helping others to fulfill theirs.

Disobedience:

This is a big one and probably the most popular of all reasons why we make detours. Disobedience is a refusal to abide by or obey the rules given by someone in authority. How many of us will admit that there have been many times that we have not done what we were told to do, whether by our parents, school teachers, our boss, or even God?

As humans, we do not always want to be told what to do. We say to ourselves, "Don't they know it's my life and I can do with it what I choose to do?", "I'm grown. I'll do what I want to do," "Who do they think they are? I got this!" or, "Why are people always in my business?" We often take offense when others begin to question our choices or try to tell us that we are making a bad decision, so the instinct on the inside of us says, "I'm going to do it anyway. I'll show them." We have built up a wall of defense and now we are caught in a trap all because we did not want to adhere to the warnings of others.

Disobedience is sin! To be disobedient to others is one thing, but disobedience to God can cost you your life. People are quick to say how much they love God, but He said in John 14:15, "If you love me, obey my commandments," (NLT). My mom would often say to me, "If you can't hear, you'll feel." She plainly meant that if I did not obey her that she would get that belt and do the discipline thing. Well, such is the same when we disobey our Heavenly Father. When we choose to be disobedient, somewhere along the line we will suffer the consequences of His judgment and His wrath.

Desperation:

Desperate people experience feelings of hopelessness and despair. They feel like their situation is a disaster, that it is impossible for it to change and that they cannot deal with the reality of what they are going through.

This is dangerous because when one is desperate he will do anything to get what he wants or to change his current situation. It could be as simple as a young child stealing a piece of candy or as dramatic as someone doing all types of devious things to get that promotion, that man or that woman. When someone feels like his back is against the wall and he does not seem to have enough money to do what he needs to do, if he is not thinking straight he could be persuaded by the enemy to steal it.

I have heard the term: "Desperate times call for desperate measures." The problem with resorting to desperate measures is that it could lead you down a path of horrible events which will eventually lead to great regret. Desperation will cause you to marry the wrong person, take any type of job, move into the worst neighborhoods, or move across the states just to get away from your family and the people who love you. It gives you the false belief that you have to do what you have to do, without realizing that there are consequences to the choices you have made during your moments of extreme despair and anguish. Desperation will definitely cause you to make detours because you become deceived into believing that you have to do what your mind and emotions are telling you to do, no matter the consequences.

Love

This is a big one because love is such a huge, broad topic. Love is a very strong emotion and it can cause us to do many things not only to get it, but to show it. British author and writer Peter Ustinov once said, "Love is an act of endless forgiveness, a tender look which becomes a habit." There is no doubt about it, love is a "many splendor thing," but these phrases exemplify the results of true love that is respected when received and unselfishly given.

Unfortunately, love is also a tool that many use in their wicked games of manipulation, deception, abuse, selfishness and perversion. The Greek philosopher Plato said these words, "Love is a serious mental disease." When channeled in the wrong way, love can become a dangerous game that people play to manipulate you into doing what they want you to do. Their selfish character will cause them to use people to their own advantage without any intention of ever returning the affection that they are given.

Unfortunately, many people mistake sex for love, so once they have had that "good roll in the hay," they are hooked on a feeling and now have the thought that, "Oh, he loves me so much." A terrible cycle begins in which someone is now being strung along while the other person reaps all the benefits. Parents are often used by their children in the name of love. The child, even the adult child, knows that Mom or Dad will do anything for him and so he plays on his parents' hearts by acting like he is so helpless and destitute when really his whole scheme is to use them to get what he wants. So often, though, the love that the parent gives is not given back to them in return.

This kind of behavior is not just limited to love relationships or parental relationships; it is in all human relationships. There will always be the givers and the takers. Love was never meant to be a tool in which we are manipulated, tricked and abused, but rather love is a gift from God that He has given to all of us freely to share and to receive. It is the easiest gift to give and it should not cost you anything. When it comes to real love, if you are treated right by others you cannot help but to reciprocate it.

French poet, dramatist and novelist Victor Hugo said this, "To love another person is to see the face of God." If a "love" relationship has taken you on a downward spiral, left you feeling hopeless, fearful, stressed out or alone, please make the decision to regain your self worth by dropping or making a change in that relationship, no matter what kind of relationship it is. Make a complete about face and run towards the One who will love you totally and unconditionally...**His name is Jesus!**

Low Self Esteem

Insecurity with oneself can cause a person to be easily persuaded to do one thing or another. People with low self-esteem go through a series of mental and emotional changes, highs and lows, ups and downs, and when these negative emotions overtake them it can lead to destructive behaviors and greatly affect their decision making.

Low self-esteem can cause someone to go through one of two extremes. Either he is extremely introverted so that he never or very rarely wants to interact with others, or he is always seeking for love and/or acceptance from others. Introverts have a hard time opening up to people, and thus they miss out on great relationships and opportunities because of their inability to trust. Their self-esteem tells them that they are safer if they stay to themselves and remain alone.

On the contrary, for some others the need to feel loved, wanted, recognized or accepted can lead to a major detour in their lives because they are now open to doing whatever it takes to feel wanted. Not everyone has the right heart, the heart of God, and so the person with low self-esteem becomes open prey to those who are only after what they can get for themselves. This is dangerous because instead of living his own life he is often used to serve, worship and cater to the one who has come to see them as a victim. Ultimately, not only does this person lose his ability to think for himself, but also the opportunity of fulfilling his own life's passion and dreams because he has been persuaded that doing for someone else is what he was created to do. That is a lie from Satan and certainly not our Heavenly Father's will for your life!

Rebellion

Well, this might be the one that sums it all up. Rebellion is defined as resistance to or defiance of any authority. Disobedience and rebellion basically fall under the same category and can have similar meanings, but rebellion takes disobedience to another level. When one is disobedient, he is refusing to comply with what was requested of him, but rebellion plainly says, "I really don't care what you say or do, I'm not going to _____" You might ask, "So, what's the danger of that?"

The Holy Scriptures say this about rebellion in **1 Samuel 15:23, "For rebellion *is as* the sin of witchcraft, and stubbornness *is as* iniquity and idolatry," (KJV).** We have to be so careful when we make choices and decisions, because whereas, "It is my life," as many say, we have to understand that we belong to God and as His creation we are to obey Him. This life that we have been blessed with was not given to us to jack up, but rather it was given to us to worship Almighty God. We are subject to His authority, so when we choose to be rebellious against His will we are sinning and that sin is as of witchcraft.

I have stated earlier in the book that God knows the plans that He has for us and those plans come together so much more easily and quickly when we allow Him to take the wheel and guide us through. There is nothing like thinking you know it all and can handle it all and then falling flat on your face only because you were too rebellious to hear sound instruction.

A Divinely Orchestrated Diversion

Would God ask you to take a detour from the path you have set for yourself?

That is a very interesting question. Until now we have discussed and viewed taking a detour in life as a negative event, but what do you do when God causes a detour in your life? Oftentimes we have our minds made up about what we want to do, how we want to do it and when we want to do it, yet the decisions we have made may not always line up with what God wants us to do. Now, that does not mean that you are necessarily doing something wrong, but maybe God has another plan for your life or He just needs you to do something different at the time.

During the summer of the year 2014, I once again tried to produce one of my plays. I had held auditions several times beginning in the year 2012 through the year 2014 trying to recast my signature play, "Murderers!", because I really wanted to do a production of it in Baltimore, but no matter how many auditions I held I still could not get a complete group of people to successfully cast the show. I was beginning to get quite discouraged.

One day as I was praying and asking God to please help me to get the people that I needed for a complete cast He asked me this question, "If I asked you to give up something that you so desperately want, would you do it?" I must admit that the question startled me for a quick moment, but without hesitation I told Him *yes*, because my heart truly seeks to please Him. Then He continued by saying, "If I asked you to give up your productions, would you do it?" Now I was quite startled and I had to really think about that. I know that God has gifted me to write and had blessed me to produce so many shows over the years, but now He was asking me *not* to pursue the one thing that I was so passionate about. It had been a few years since I had produced a full-length play and the thought of doing it again had been on my mind for quite some time. Sure, I had done a few skits here and there and had produced a few artistic variety shows, but that was not enough. Besides, I thought that this was what God wanted me to do and several people kept advising me that I needed to get back to producing my plays.

Almighty God continued by saying to me, "I need you to focus on ministry right now and trying to produce this show is becoming a major distraction from what I need you to do." Wow! It was at that moment that I understood why I was having such a struggle with this particular project. It was not that I could not find the right people to cast or produce a really great show. It was actually God blocking it because He needed me to focus my attention on building my church and doing some work in other areas of ministry to which He has called me. I did not realize at that time the elevation that was about to come and the next assignment that He had for me. I also must admit that at that moment, when I made the declaration to God that I would do whatever He wanted me to do, I felt a huge weight lift up off my shoulders. The truth is that I actually felt more and more like a failure each time I had put so much work into the audition process only to have nothing come of it.

"Then he said to them all: Whoever wants to be my disciple must deny themselves and take up their cross daily and follow me," Luke 9:23, NIV.

God was asking me to take a detour, a turn, a temporary deviation from my desires and what I wanted to do to fulfill what He needed me to do. He did not say that I would never do another production, but it certainly was not going to be then. That is what I call a divinely orchestrated detour that comes with great rewards and benefits, because obedience to Almighty God always pays off. We must also know that just because something does not manifest when we want it to does not mean that we have been denied, but rather it has only been delayed.

So many times we get upset with God when things do not go as *we* have planned, not realizing that He is only trying to spare us from something and if we are willing to be truthful we will admit that there have been times when we have ignored God and did what we wanted to do anyway. Yet, God is so merciful and so kind that He will often block a situation, not because He is *not* for you, but because He *is* for you. We humans like to really stretch our power of free will. We take it to the limit and we will push and push and push against the grain (God's will) until we make things happen. Sometimes we act as if God is our enemy, that He is against us and does not want us to have anything. Wow, sounds like a spoiled brat having a tantrum, doesn't it?

Now, let's not get confused. Yes, God has placed inside of you a desire, a passion and a need to succeed, to gain and bear fruit. Oh yes, all of that is true. We cannot help it. It was part of the construction plan when He was creating you that you would want to become more than you are and obtain more than what you have, but you must also remember that your Creator knows what you want and need. He knows us better than we know ourselves. Almighty God looks ahead and can see what is in front of you so He, being merciful, will intervene at the right time to prevent a head on collision if you allow Him. Even more encouraging is that since God created you, He also knows what great things He has in store for you. If He did not divert us sometimes and interrupt our plans we would self-destruct and totally miss out on the blessings, that perfect husband or wife, the best opportunities, the job suited just for us and any other predestined benefits that He has for us.

Is it always easy to accept God's will? No. It is not always easy, but it is always best! Because of God's undying, unconditional love for you, He only wants the best for you and nothing that you may or may not do will ever separate you from His love. Consider what it says in Romans 8:38-39, **"For I am persuaded that neither death nor life, nor angels nor principalities nor powers, nor things present nor things to come, nor height nor depth, nor any other created thing, shall be able to separate us from the love of God which is in Christ Jesus our Lord," (NKJV).**

Your Heavenly Father loves you so much that He will let nothing separate you from His love. Even when you sin and make terrible choices, He still loves you. Remember, God hates sin, but He does not hate you. We still have to be careful not to continue in those things that we know are of offense to Him and against His will. In the previous chapter I spoke of rebellion being as the sin of witchcraft. Never be so adamant or determined that you must have your way that you make the mistake of falling into the hands of an angry God. Do not be so rebellious and disobedient that you cause yourself to forfeit God's favor and blessings that He has prepared for you. Trust me, He knows a whole lot more than you know and He can make your life wonderful, joyous and ultimately fulfilling if you would just yield your all to Him. Make up in your heart and mind that you will get out of the way and let God have His way in your life.

What has God been asking you to divert from? What has He been blocking that you keep trying to push past? Who has God allowed to walk away from you that you keep chasing after? What doors has He closed that you are determined to try and reopen? He has been lovingly sparing you from destruction, but you keep fighting Him. Have you asked God lately what He would have you to do? Are you afraid of His answer? True, He may say *no* to some things or to that someone that you really want, but have the courage and boldness to say to yourself, "In spite of that, not my will Father, but Thy will be done." You were created to bring Him glory and honor and how you live your life, the life He gave you, determines if you do or not. My mind reflects on the very heartfelt and precious words of David in Psalm 23:1-6:

> **The Lord is my shepherd; I shall not want. He maketh me to lie down in green pastures: He leadeth me beside the still waters. He restoreth my soul: He leadeth me in the paths of righteousness for His name's sake. Yea, though I walk through the valley of the shadow of death, I will fear no evil: for Thou art with me; Thy rod and Thy staff they comfort me. Thou preparest a table before me in the presence of mine enemies: Thou anointest my head with oil; my cup**

runneth over. Surely goodness and mercy shall follow me all the days of my life: and I will dwell in the house of the LORD forever. (KJV)

I encourage you with these words: Allow God to lead and guide you. Allow Him to take control of the wheel as you navigate through life. He knows the road and the way that you take. He has the master plan that brings you to a successful end. The plan that Almighty God has for you is great and it is not like anyone else's. Do not allow people to influence you away from being obedient to what He wants you to do, because when things do not turn out just right those same people will be the first to criticize you. They will also be MIA (Missing in Action) when you need someone to help you get out of a tight spot. Obey the Lord! Allow Him to guide you and you will make it safely to your preordained, predestined destination.

I'm Ready, Lord

Take my hand, Precious Lord
I heard the song say,
But when You tried to do just that
I went another way.
I want to fulfill my destiny, my purpose on
this earth
But how will I ever do that if
I don't consult you first.
Lead me Lord, I'll follow, I've said so many times
But my own way and my own choices
Have left me empty and hollow.
So take my hand, Precious Lord
Please, I'm asking You once again
I'll give you all of me this time
Dear Master, Lord and Friend!

Shawna C. Branch

It's Time to Turn Around

While reading this book you may have reflected on a time or several times that you have made the wrong choice or decision in your life. You may have found yourself lost in a maze of confusion, wonderment and fear. Maybe you found yourself in despair, embarrassment, shame, or left alone to deal with the consequences of a detour you have made in your life. I want to encourage you to know that no matter how bad it looks to you right now, you can begin again and turn that situation around.

Our loving Father, Almighty God, is waiting for you to come to Him. Bring Him your problems, be honest about how and why you are on the road you are on and He will help you to get back on the right track. You must be willing to be honest and accept responsibility for your mistakes. Denial will delay your deliverance! It does not even really matter how you got off track or why you made the choices you have made. Again, you were created to bring God glory, so when you mess up and realize that you tried to be in control when only He is in control, the words, "Please forgive me, Lord," sound so sweet to His ears. Do not let pride block you from being free.

"But He said to me, 'My grace is sufficient for you, for my power is made perfect in weakness.' Therefore, I will boast all the more gladly about my weaknesses, so that Christ's power may rest on me," (2 Corinthians 12:9).

God knows your heart, yes, but He also needs you to be willing to admit your faults and then He is faithful to forgive you of all unrighteousness. Your life is not over; rather, it is just beginning. I am so thankful that although God permitted my marriage, He did not allow the experiences to overtake me and destroy me while I was in the marriage. Yes, I loved my husband, but that does not mean that we were meant to be husband and wife. God gave us both what we wanted and I do not regret any of it, yet I know that it was His mercy and grace that spared my life. God knows what is best for us, but we keep telling Him what we are going to do instead of asking Him, "Lord, what would you have me to do?" Love is beautiful and marriage is honorable, but anything done out of the perfect will of God will ultimately become a disaster.

I realize that we are human and as humans we will make many mistakes. Some will be minor, but some will be major and it will appear that we cannot correct our huge mess-ups. On the contrary, this is what God's Word tells us:

> **"If we confess our sins, He is faithful and just and will forgive us our sins and purify us from all unrighteousness," (1 John 1:9).**

It does not matter how long you have been on the wrong path — that deserted path, a path of arrogance, pride and disobedience — you can start over and still fulfill your purpose in the kingdom of God. Grab hold of God, seek His face and see that He bring you out victorious. Too often we commit and dedicate ourselves to everyone else. It is time to commit, submit and dedicate yourself to God. He is the only one who truly has your best interest at heart. People will promise you the world, and with good intentions they will do their best to be there for you. However, God is the only one who will never, ever leave you, disappoint you, quit on you, ignore you, lie to you, cheat on you, degrade you, mishandle you, use you, abuse you, make fun of you, or bully you. He will not try to manipulate you or make you feel guilty, nor will He promise you something and then not make good on His Word.

Think about it, please. It is time to stop running and diverting from the path that is best for your life. It is time to stop being tricked and fooled by the devil and his imps. It is time to stop feeling like you are less and realize that you are somebody in God's eyes. Decide that you will no longer believe any negative reports, but rather you will believe the report of the

Lord. His report says that you are beautiful, you are intelligent, you are cared for, and you are somebody! His report says that you are His child. God loves us with an undying, unconditional love. He wants the best for us and will do His best for us. It is time to let your heavenly Father know that you love Him too and the best way to show Him is to be obedient to His Word and His will for your life. The best is yet to come! It is not over yet. It is not over until God says it is over and the outcome is in His hand.

"And we know that in all things God works for the good of those who love Him, who have been called according to His purpose," (Romans 8:28).

What has God told you to do that you have not yet done? Where has He asked you to go that you have not yet gone? What instructions have you been given that you have chosen to ignore? Ask yourself this question: "What am I running from?" Your destiny is important. Your destiny is the predestined, preordained life that God set for you even before the world began. Before you were formed in your mother's womb, he already knew how your life would go. You see, we make all of these decisions and very adamantly declare what we will or will not do without realizing that God knew all the while what we would or would not do.

"No temptation has overtaken you except what is common to mankind. And God is faithful; He will not let you be tempted beyond what you can bear. But when you are tempted, He will also provide a way out so that you can endure it," (1 Corinthians 10:13).

Do you think that any decision you have made or will make in the future is a surprise to God? No sir, no ma'am. God is the Creator of all and Father of all. He knows every single thing about you and your life. From the cradle to the grave, He knows it all, so you are not doing anything unusual when you make the decision to have it your way. He knew all along what you would do and yet He allowed you to do it anyway, and better than that He protected you while you were in it.

Beloved, if you have found yourself in a detour, on a path that has caused you to divert from your original destination, I want to strongly urge you to repent, seek God's forgiveness and make the decision to turn around. You can begin again. As long as there is breath in your body, you still have an opportunity to change the course of your life. You do not have to stay in bondage, nor do you have to be under anyone's control. Take a step in the right direction and regain control of your destiny. The life that Almighty God prepared for you before the foundation of the world is still available to you!

Restoration Has Come

We serve a merciful and gracious God. He loves us in spite of our choices, in spite of our behavior and in spite of our disobedience to Him. Many have entered into the detour zone of their lives and did not make it out, but I thank God that although I experienced many life-threatening challenges, I made it! Almighty God brought me through.

My choices led me to a very dark place. I have experienced living in a home that became a crack house and the loss of all my precious possessions. I have come face to face with drug dealers and addicts, had money stolen from me and eventually became homeless. I lost the respect of many, and close friends walked away from me because they did not want to deal with me and my "problem." I found myself in a sea of poverty; no money anywhere, no way to pay my bills, in debt like crazy owing landlords, banks, and other creditors. Oh, it got terrible. In all of that I had lost the one thing that I knew God Himself had given me — my gift, my talent, my writing. I did not know what to do to get it back. I was empty and could not feel any inspiration anywhere.

In 2011, after Bobby's death, I began to yearn for my gift again. I wanted to write something so badly. I wanted to produce plays again. I loved who I was when I was writing or acting and I desperately wanted it back. I prayed and repented and prayed and repented some more because I began to face the reality that no matter what had happened over the past ten years of my life, it was my decision to let go of the gift!

I prayed and asked God to restore me and He did. In May 2011, I wrote a skit called "I Cried Lord, Lord!" It tells the story of a rambunctious evangelist who finds herself left behind after the rapture. It is a one woman, one act play. I first performed it at the America's Best Inn on Frankford Avenue in Baltimore, Maryland and I still perform it once a year. After writing that skit and performing it a few times my appetite for writing was ignited once again. I had to write. I had to perform.

I prayed for God to connect me with people in the Baltimore area who were interested in performing and the answer to my prayer came one day when I met a young, energetic, outgoing young man named Kyron. He mentioned that he was an aspiring actor. I approached him after the class we were attending and we set out to do some things together. It was through him that God fully restored my gift! The excitement that this young man had was contagious. He would introduce me to so many young people who wanted to perform and together we all did a few productions.

I share this because it is important for you to know that just because you make a detour and just because things seem to take a terrible turn, it is never too late to begin again. It is never too late to start over and reach your destiny or fulfill your dreams. I am so thankful that the detour in my life came to an end and that I found my way back on the right course; the predestined and preordained course that my Father had set for my life. Thank you, Jesus!

Challenges and life's circumstances will always come, but the key is to never give up, no matter what you have to face. Do not give up and do not quit! Had I totally given up and thrown in the towel I would never have met the wonderful people who are in my life today and I certainly would not be living the blessed life that I am living. God is a restorer of all things broken! He is a restorer of life, purpose, will and opportunity. His undying, unconditional love for us causes Him to reach way down and pluck us up out of our mess. After we have learned the lessons and been through the fire, He places us on solid ground and gives us another chance to get it right.

My heart is grateful to Almighty God for allowing me to go through my experiences and make it out, not just with my life, but with my right mind. You see, another important point is because the detour zone can be a very dark place, your mind and emotions are greatly affected. During my year of living homeless in my car there were many nights that I felt like I was going to lose my mind. Freezing cold sometimes, burning hot sometimes, starving hungry many times and terribly afraid all the time! Yet in all of that God kept my mind. He kept my mind and He restored my soul.

I have learned so much over the last fifteen years, more than I would ever have thought I would. If I had to make a list of all the things that I got out of my experience and if anyone asked me to name the one thing that I am most thankful for, at the top of the list would be that I am so thankful for my relationship with God. It was during the darkest times and the hardest days of my life that my relationship with God was being built and fortified and that is something that no one can ever take from me: my personal relationship with God. It is greater than any other relationship that I have had or will ever have with anyone else in life. His love is so much more real and understandable to me. His tender care is so much more precious to me. The fact that He is an ultimate protector and provider is so mind blowing to me. It is amazing that He forgives us when we finally come to our senses and repent of our wrong doings in spite of our rebellion and our disobedience. In spite of it all, He still forgives us and throws that sin into the sea of forgetfulness, never to remember it anymore.

God is a restorer of all things broken. Once we were broken, yet now we are made whole. There is an exit to your detour. When you find it, drive quickly and get back on track. The road ends — yes, every road ends — but you have the power to decide how and where it ends. Take the hand of the Restorer, switch lanes and make it safely to your destiny. To God be the Glory!

References

The Merriam-Webster Dictionary: All words defined were taken from the Merriam Webster Dictionary

New International Version Bible: All scriptural quotes were taken from the NIV, KJV and NKJV versions of the Holy Bible